# I Am Worth It!

## How to Set Your Price and other Advice for Freelancers

JT Hine

Printed and bound in the United States of America.

Publisher:
Scriptor Services LLC
PO Box 4623
Charlottesville, Virginia 22905-4623 USA

**Library of Congress Cataloging-in-Publication Data.**

Hine, JT, 2017, 2020.
I Am Worth It! /JT Hine
29 pp. 22 cm.
1. Self-employed. 2. Small business – Management.
I. Hine, JT II. Title
HD8036.H45 2020
ISBN – 978-1-7331755-6-2 (eBook)
ISBN – 978-1-7331755-7-9 (Paperback)

# Contents

# INTRODUCTION

**MARIO PUSHED BACK HIS CHAIR**, rubbed his eyes, and reached for another sip of Computer De-Stress tea.

"It's done, Cindy," he said, clicking the "Save" icon on the income tax return file.

"So, big refund, or big tax bill?" his wife asked, without looking up from her proofreading at the big table in their shared office.

"Refund," he said. "Big one."

"Let me see." Cindy came around to Mario's computer screen. "Why so big?"

"Because it's time to go full-time, that's why," said Mario. "Look at this." He brought up the spreadsheet with the summary of their revenue for the last year. "See? We are equaling both our day-jobs now. And that is just translating half-time. Just think what we could do if we put the whole work-week into the business. We are both turning down more work than we can take in."

She put her hands on his shoulders and stood behind him, staring at the screen. She seemed lost in thought for a while.

"I think you're right. It's the second year in a row we have matched our salaries."

"And that is when we said we would make the move."

"How fast?"

"All according to plan," Mario said. "But this time next year, the company picnic will just be the two of us."

Cindy still looked at the screen. "We have worked so hard for so long to get to this point, I can't believe we have really made it. I feel like it sneaked up on us."

Mario gasped as she tickled his ribs, sharply, suddenly. He leapt us as she laughed and ran from the room. He shouted in mock anger, laughing as he chased her across the house...

**Freelancers are a varied lot.** Some are just starting out, with no work experience. Others perhaps are long-service employees recently retired or "re-structured." Some are single, some have working partners, and some are suddenly alone for whatever reason.

"Going freelance" is fun. It is exciting. It is often scary. It is stressful, but the rewards can make it worthwhile. Not just the money – there is the satisfaction, the independence, the self-respect. Whatever work you do, if you hope people will pay you for it, you are in business. And if you own a small business or freelance, it can feel very lonely sometimes.

**Probably the toughest question starting out:** "What should I charge for my work?" There are many ways to answer that question. This book will examine just one: calculating a realistic minimum rate. In the world of business, we call it the *break-even point*. Above it, we are making a profit; below it, we are giving our work away.

We may calculate our minimum price anytime, but we should do so at least whenever major changes occur in our financial situation or expectations. We need to have the figures ready before the customer calls or walks in. Knowing the minimum price ahead of time not only helps us decide whether to accept an assignment, but it also helps in developing the estimate when requested.

There are other considerations in setting our prices, such as the difficulty of the work, the demand for our particular service, and other market-based factors. These are beyond the scope of this book. However, because of these considerations, we should keep our individual minimum prices to ourselves. It is not the sort of number we should place on the Internet or in our advertising. The minimum should be something less than the lower end of any range we do publish or advertise.

We may need to turn down an assignment for several reasons, including unsuitability of the job, the conditions, not being able to meet the deadline or conflicting prior commitments. On the other hand, there are excellent reasons for taking on work that does not pay enough. For example, we might build good will with a new client, do scholarly research that is important to us, or work for a favorite charity or a relative. Knowing whether a particular assignment will make or lose money should figure in the decision.

**Is this book for you?** I wrote this book to help freelancers of any kind. The emphasis is on service providers whose work has intangible value (no physical product). However, in the case of crafters, artists and others whose output appears tangible, the time and intangible value in their products often far outweighs the value of the materials involved. You, too, can use the techniques in this book to make sure you charge enough for each item.

As you learn to calculate your break-even point, you should start organizing yourself to think and act like a business owner. Budgeting, taxes, organization – these are all part of the freelance business. There is even a "payroll" to calculate – yours!

# 1. BEING IN BUSINESS

ANYONE WHO REGULARLY OFFERS A PRODUCT or a service for consideration is in business. To stay in business, enough money needs to come in to cover costs and return a profit.

Before looking at the work from a business perspective, we need to evaluate it from a technical point of view (Is it in my field? Can I handle the quantity by myself? Can I meet the deadline? How much of it can I finish by the given deadline?). Once we know we can do the work, we should look at the money.

Revenue is not the most important reason for accepting or rejecting a piece. Most of us freelancers do what we do because we love it. Each of us alone knows what value to place on the money and the satisfaction of the work. It is very liberating, however, to know that something we want to do anyway will not cost the family budget and may help it. There are also some assignments that are not as attractive as others: knowing whether they make or lose money can ease the decision one way or the other.

Here are some basic business principles that apply to small business, especially freelancing.

## 1.1 Principle 1: We are in it for the money.

Charles Kulp is a slender, pleasant man. He wears thin-rimmed glasses and can listen intently. Counseling small businesses takes a lot of listening. A sign on the wall behind him, in plain view of his clients, keeps the counseling sessions focused and pointed:

***If you are not in business for the money ...***

***You are not in business.***

Neil Inglis observed that submission to a "poverty cult" can be harmful to our economic health.[1] Failure to recognize the value of what we do can stall us as individuals and as professionals.

If we total our needs accurately and completely, the rate obtained by the break-even method will tell us how much revenue is enough. That will drive other business decisions, such as whether to get a better-paying day job, increase our marketing efforts, or redirect our efforts to profitable areas and away from losers.

One of the most important business decisions we can make is to get out of a business. A proper analysis may reveal that we will never break even. If we truly love our work, we may find it very liberating to stop trying to make it pay its way. We could take on the research of the family records or re-translate a beloved author for pleasure - and really enjoy it. We could do volunteer work with social agencies or non-profits. We could go to fairs and markets for the fun of it when we can or want to, and not worry about "covering the cost."

## 1.2 Principle 2: We charge for expertise, not product.

The difference between a professional or artisan and a semi-skilled wage laborer is expertise. Whatever our field,

---

[1] Neil Inglis, "A Taste of Armageddon: Facing the Challenges of the New Millennium," Address at the East Coast Regional Conference of the American Translators Association, Washington, June 1, 1996.

we are doing something that not everyone can do. Customers are willing to pay to make that expertise available.

Service providers, such as writers, translators, therapists, instructors, and day-care providers, should not confuse products and something that contracting officers call *deliverables*. Certainly physical "products" seem to exchange hands in the form of money, manuscripts, reports, objects, and electronic files. In the marketplace of words and ideas, the value of such tangible signs is irrelevant. As independent contractors, freelancers are paid to submit their deliverables on time, but the value – and the price paid – depends on the intangible content rather than the medium of transmission.

It is not much of a leap to realize that the intangible value of a hand-made bowl or a quilt is far greater than the cost of the materials in it.

## 1.3 Principle 3: We are really selling time-based units of our expertise.

Because we are selling a skilled service rather than a product, we must measure the service appropriately. Professionals usually charge for their expertise in units of *time*. For that matter, any form of labor only makes sense economically if measured in time units. That is why we express salaries and wages in monthly, weekly or hourly units. Even when the worker is paid by the piece – for example the rate per basket or kilogram paid to migrant farm workers – the amount paid depends on the worker's expected speed. Speed is a time-based unit.

## 1.4 Principle 4: We should separate the business from other sources of income and expenditure.

This is just good advice, but it may trip up more would-be businesspeople than almost anything else, especially home-based freelancers. The identity of the business must be distinct in the minds of the owner and everyone associated with the business (colleagues, customers, etc.). A business by definition must be a *going concern*, which implies a certain personality of its own. Incorporation is not necessary, but there are several things you can do to give your business its own identity.

One way is to register what is called a *fictitious name* for your business. It could be as simple as "Trading As [My Name], [occupation]." This is usually done at the local courthouse or civil registry office. In some countries, the Chamber of Commerce registers businesses. Find out if your locality requires you to have a business license and pay your taxes. A separate credit card for business charges is a good idea. It could be a personal card kept for that purpose.

A separate business checking account and credit card can reduce your bookkeeping. Paying by check creates a record of each transaction in the register. The combination of a well-kept checkbook register, credit card statements, and a small notebook for cash transactions may be all the "books" that a self-employed professional needs for a long time.

Money from non-business sources (like the other job) goes into the business checking account if the business needs it. The owner takes money from the business account when necessary. These transactions in and out of the business must be clear and traceable. Money going into the business account is called *owner's contribution*. Money coming out for personal use is called *owner's draw*.

In the beginning, outside sources of income have to pay for business operating expenses like paper or capital equipment like the computer. It is important to keep track of these expenses. If you can, try not to buy things for the business with personal money. Instead, put the money into the business checking account as needed. For example, if you have a separate credit card for the business, you can make an owner's contribution into the business checking account just before paying the credit card statement.

If you are using accounting software (e.g., Quicken, Quickbooks, Freshbooks, Microsoft Money, Mint ), you can "separate" personal and business money by using unique category names for business and personal income and expenses. For example, all categories relating to the business can have an "S-" in front to the name. The letter is arbitrary. When sorting reports, or viewing income and expenses, it is easy to select only personal or only business categories.

# 2. CALCULATING YOUR NEEDS

TO CALCULATE HOW MUCH to charge a customer you first must know how much money you need. This means you must build a budget for the business.

Preparing a business budget highlights the importance of separating personal and business finances. It may surprise you to learn how much you have been subsidizing the business from other income.

A freelancer's business budget has three major components.

Personal Budget (Labor). As a freelancer, you are the only "employee" in the business, so employee-type categories go here: income to live on (your "pay"), estimated taxes, retirement set-asides, life insurance, etc.

Business Operating Budget. A business needs money of its own to survive.

Growth and Capitalization. Any business must earn enough money to buy the equipment and material it needs to expand, and to replace what wears out.

## 2.1 The Personal Budget

Whether you work full time or part time, you must calculate a complete budget for yourself and your family. All spending and all desired future purchases go into the budget, not just survival items.

**Anything you *want* is a *need* in this personal budget.**

Obviously, you may need several runs at this after comparing what you want with what you can earn. Eventually, however, you can figure out how much the business must yield as its share of the family income. This amount becomes the only connection between the personal finances and the business finances. It is the amount of owner's draw you will take out of the business.

## 2.2 The Business Operating Budget

This budget includes the business telephone bill, Internet Service Provider (ISP), paper and office supplies, vehicle and travel expenses, advertising, postage stamps, photocopying, etc. The forms used to submit business income tax returns can serve as a convenient list of categories (for example, Schedule C of IRS Form 1040 in the USA).

Beware of common pitfalls when drawing up a business budget. One is the tendency to shortchange the business. When first starting out, the amounts of money may seem so high that they tempt you to economize during the budgeting process. Do not cut corners until after all you have all your business needs written out. Do not even look at potential revenue during this phase. Later, what you cannot afford becomes part of your growth plan; you must identify what you need first, then plan to achieve it.

Another mistake is to overlook familiar expenses. For example, business cards are an advertising expense. Postage should be a noticeable number. If not, family stamps may be mixed with the business stamps. You may have internet service and TV or telephone from the same provider: the internet service part of that provider's bill is a business expense if it is the backbone of your home office.

Like postage, it is easy to overlook business telephone expenses, especially if you have not yet set up a separate telephone number for the business. During the year, you should go through each phone bill and keep track of business calls as if there were a separate business line into the house. Don't forget the taxes and charges on those calls. I used a highlighter on the phone bills then totaled up the business portions on each one until I could afford a separate telephone line for the business. That land-line supported the fax machine and served as a dial-up backup for voice and internet when the power went out. Today, I have a generous data allowance on my cell phone to keep the office running without power.

If you use your personal automobile in your business, decide how to report car and truck expenses on your taxes and use the same system for your budget. The Tax Codes in some countries allow a deduction for either mileage or actual expenses.

Find out if the Tax Code in your country distinguishes between business travel and commuting. It is business travel if you bill the client for it, especially if it shows on the invoice. It is business travel if you do not work on site, but simply pick up assignments or meet people and bring the work back to the home office. But it may be commuting if:

- you sign a contract to work on-site for an extended time, and
- the client does not pay for the daily trip to the site, and
- you are not making rounds to other customers during the day.

In some countries (like the USA), commuting is not deductible as a business expense. Get professional tax advice if you need more information.

## 2.3 Growth and Capitalization

A business is like an organism. If an organism does not grow, it dies. Just keeping income steady requires growth planning to meet customers' expectations and to replace customers that move on. The cost of things usually rises. The business must keep up with inflation.

Depending on your field, the growth budget could contain:

- a faster, more powerful computer;
- a new smartphone;
- new software;
- the cost of moving to a larger office or improvements to the old one;
- a fax machine, scanner, copier or all-in-one;
- books you borrow often from the library but hope to buy some day;
- tools you rent often;
- installation charges for a business telephone or internet service account;
- the cost of developing a website;
- anything you need or want for the business but you do not have now.

This is a list of one-time expenses, not regular operating costs. Thus, "new smartphone" means the cost of the cellular telephone and the installation of service, not the monthly bill or the cost of new batteries. After you purchase a cellular phone, the monthly service becomes part of the Business Operating Budget.

Once you have the list of what you need to grow, you price it out and figure out when you need to buy each item. Then it becomes clear how much money you need to amass each year toward the purchases.

There are some things almost all freelancers need to perform competently, like a computer, printer/copier, internet service, and software. If you go to customer locations (like a landscaper or a cleaning service), you may need a commercial or specialized vehicle in addition to the family car.

Don't let your growth plan become too complicated: budget for the things you really need now and include a growth factor for the rest. After setting aside money for taxes at the end of the year, you can buy items on the growth list as the cash reserve allows.

## 2.4. Pulling It Together: The Business Budget

Table 1 below pulls together the personal, operating and growth budgets into a single sheet for the business.

These figures are completely hypothetical. If the business is the only source of income, the "Portion coming from other sources" is zero. You do this also when you are testing to see if you can afford to leave the "day job."

You would also put any asset income (dividends, trust income, pension from former career, etc.) in the "Portion coming from other sources." If your spouse or partner works outside the business, show that income in "Portion coming from other sources." Any hours your spouse or partner contributes to your business will be added to your hours.

A word about depreciation (amortization). Some large pieces of equipment (*capital items*, e.g., computer, kiln, automobile) may need to be depreciated, with only part of their value deducted from gross revenues each year. In some countries, there are generous limits under which a freelancer or small business owner can simply *expense* capital items, deducting the whole cost against that year's revenues. Regardless of your tax situation, I recommend keeping a line for depreciation in the business budget, in order to build a fund to replace expensive items. Call it a "sinking fund" if you like, but plan to save money to replace the computer, the kiln or the automobile. This is not the same thing as saving to buy something new. This line simply recognizes that everything wears out some day.

This is not only one way to assemble a business budget. You could also replace the entire Personal Budget portion of the worksheet with a "desired salary." This number would be the value of your day job, or any portion of the family income that you want the business to supply.[2]

[2] Claude Whitmyer and Salli Rasberry, *Running A One-Person Business*, Berkeley: Ten-Speed Press, 1994.

| ITEM | MONTH | YEAR |
|---|---|---|
| **Personal Budget**: | | |
| Rent/house payment | 525 | $6,300 |
| Groceries | 400 | $4,800 |
| Insurance (life, health, etc.) | 250 | $3,000 |
| Clothing | 125 | $1,500 |
| Vehicle fuel, repairs | 60 | $ 720 |
| Charitable pledges | 90 | $1,080 |
| Eating out | 120 | $1,440 |
| Vacation | 125 | $1,500 |
| Utilities | 250 | $3,000 |
| Retirement account | 188 | $2,256 |
| Other (hobbies, school, etc.) | 220 | $2,640 |
| ***Sub-total: personal budget*** | | **$28,236** |
| ***Portion coming from other sources*** | 686 | $8,236 |
| ***OWNER'S DRAW REQUIRED*** | | **$ 20,000** |
| **Business Operating Budget** | | |
| Advertising | 10 | $ 120 |
| Vehicle (mileage) | 120 | $1,440 |
| Fees | 15 | $ 180 |
| Depreciation (amortization) | 350 | $4,200 |
| Office expense | 10 | $ 120 |
| Rent | 150 | $1,800 |
| Supplies | 100 | $1,200 |
| Utilities | 110 | $1,320 |
| Dues | 40 | $ 480 |
| Other (Postage, books, training, etc.) | 75 | $ 900 |
| ***Sub-total: business operating*** | | **$11,760** |
| ***Personal budget*** | | $20,000 |
| ***Sub-Total*** | | **$31,760** |
| **Growth (3%)** | | **$ 953** |
| ***TOTAL REQUIREMENT*** | | **$32,713** |

Table 1– Business Budget Worksheet

Be careful when comparing your business income to your day job. Remember to add the value of any employee benefits to your salary or wage. This can be either what your employer spends on you (including the contributions that are not shown in your pay stub), or you can calculate what it would cost you to replace those benefits (health plan, insurance, pension, Social Security contribution, etc.). For example, I compared my employer's and my spouse's employer's health and retirement plans to a package of group insurance plans, plus an Individual Retirement Account, plus mutual fund investing for retirement. For a while, my employer was sending me to school, so I had to count the cost of tuition and fees when deciding if I could afford to go into full time freelance work.

The business tax forms are a helpful starting point, but they cannot adequately capture all the real expenses of a business. You should add whatever accounts you need to track the expenses of your particular business.

There is a lot of help available for freelancers and home-office operators. The local library should have books about running your own business. Some cities have Small Business Development Centers or local schools may offer courses or consultation for starting a business. The internet also has a wealth of information and electronic bookstores for the self-help books. The US Small Business Administration (https://www.sba.gov/) has a wealth of information, and the principles behind their publications are useful generally, in case you are not in the United States.

Now that you know how much you need to collect, you can assign a value to the productive hours that you can bill.

# 3. DETERMINING AN HOURLY RATE

WHETHER EXPRESSED as an hourly rate or not, the amount on your invoice should be a function of your time.

To set the billable rate correctly, divide your total income requirement by the number of billable hours in a year. There are not as many working hours in a year as might appear at first.

For example, here is a typical breakdown used by a personnel administrator in Virginia:

| Conditions | Hours/year |
|---|---|
| 52 weeks @ 40 hours/week (full-time) | 2080 |
| *Less* a two-week vacation (80 hours) | 2000 |
| *Less* eleven holidays (8 hours/day) | 1912 |
| *Less* allowance for sick time (10 hours/month) | 1792 |
| *Less* overhead (indirect costs) (e.g., 30%) | **1255** |

Table 2 – Finding the Number of Billable Hours in a Work-year.

If you are going to work part-time (less than 40 hours/week), you enter Table 2 with a lower number: whatever the total hours you can devote to the business in a year. Then calculate what percentage of full time the total is, then apply that percentage to the holiday and sick time in Table 2. If you are working for someone else, you might find it convenient to use the allocations for holidays and sick time that your employer uses.

Self-employed businesspeople have control over how many holidays they take and how many hours of sick leave they need to budget. They can fine-tune those lines better than an employer or personnel expert can.

However, avoid the common mistake of working all the time. Those whose businesses survive learn to take their holidays and vacations. Also, freelancers who do not budget holidays, time off to be sick and non-billable overhead will charge less than their time is worth.

**Working on holidays to make a deadline is a *part* of life; it should not become a *way* of life.**

The hours spent on the business for the benefit of all clients (research, travel, marketing, training, etc.) are as important as the time on each project. The way we account for work for several clients or all of them is called *indirect cost allocation*. Customers pay for all hours spent directly on their projects and a fair share of the hours spent on indirect costs. Indirect costs include shopping for office supplies, handling e-mail, taking deposits to the bank, paying bills and other activities that apply to the whole business, not just a particular job.

The arbitrary thirty percent used in Table 2 would equate to working one hour on non-billable activities for every two hours spent directly on a particular customer's job.

Indirect costs are also known as *overhead*. They are often misunderstood, but they are as much a part of the business as the direct labor. The point is to track the time spent on indirect activities carefully and to make sure that it stays reasonable and on task. Anyone running a business, including your customers, should understand indirect costs and expect them in the rates. Nevertheless, the subject rarely comes up in rate negotiations.

Using the formula

*Labor Rate = (Income Requirement) / (Billable Hours)*

we find that our hypothetical freelancer in Tables 1 and 2 must bill at least $26.07/hour. It would be normal to use the next-higher whole number as our break-even point, or $27/hour in this example.

Clearly this is a personal exercise, so there will always be a wide range in the lowest level of remuneration each of us can accept. If you just left military service or college without major personal debts, you may be able to take an offer that someone with more experience might have to turn down. That senior colleague may have acquired a graduate school loan, children, and a mortgage along with the value-added professional experience.

None of this has anything to do with what the market will bear. Clearly if your service is in great demand you can command higher rates than those whose services are more commonly available. There is a premium for quality, too. We all get that one chance to make a first impression. Customers learn that it is worth some money to cultivate contractors who work quickly and meet their deadlines with good-looking work that does not need re-doing. You can (and should) perform market research as you work. Those techniques are beyond the scope of this book, because they vary so much from one profession to the next.

Break-even analysis of this sort can help you with plans and decision-points. For example, you could set milestones in your business plan to have the business break even in three years and grow 3% each year after that. You could also determine what sort of regular freelance income you would need to be able to leave your day job.

# 4. THE PIECE RATE

TRANSLATORS, CRAFTERS AND many other freelancers have to sell their products or services by the item, regardless of the number of hours of work. It might be euros per page, cents per word, or dollars per bowl, blouse or anything else. In labor management, we call this kind of pricing a *piece rate*. (If you normally bill by the hour, you do not have to find your piece rate.)

Conversion from hourly rate to piece rate involves

- estimating how many hours the job will take,
- multiplying by the hourly rate to estimate the total quote for the job, then
- dividing by the estimated number of words, lines, baskets, pots or whatever, to arrive at a piece rate to quote to the customer.

The key to a good estimate is knowing how long the job will take. This is why translators insist on seeing a sample before quoting a job, and technical writers want to see the product before writing the user manual. Landscapers can't give an estimate without visiting the site. Each freelancer's working style and skill set are unique, so each has a different output per hour on a given task.

To learn your personal speed, you must time your work. In addition to recording how much time you spend on overhead activities, it is important to keep the clock running when working in any way on a job. Proofreading, finishing and return visits to the job site can affect the revenue-per-hour rate of the finished job considerably. Producing work of acceptable quality requires enough time to make sure that the job is perfect and that the customer is satisfied. The extra time is part of the job.

Not only is each freelancer's basic production rate highly variable, but other factors affect the time required for a job. Here are some reasons why the piece rate may go up or down:

- research to prepare the estimate or the job;
- finding special tools, references or materials;
- sub-contracting specialized or temporary help;
- language expansion factor (translators);
- graphics or formatting (any word-worker);
- delivery (electronic, paper, hand-delivered?);
- travel requirements.

These and many other things can add to the cost of a job. You should warn customers about time-consuming work that does not call directly on the skill for which they need you. Sometimes the customer can take on parts of the project that do not require your expertise. If you handle it properly, most customers appreciate your working with them to get the most for their money. At the same time, you get to spend your time doing what you like and not something that someone else can do better. I never met a customer who did not appreciate my helping them save money. They show it by sending me more work.

Sometimes the extras get so complicated that it becomes impossible to figure them into a piece rate. When that happens, you should probably try to show such extras separately in the contract or purchase order and charge an hourly fee for them. If you can, give the customer a rough estimate, expressed as a maximum. Be conservative in your own favor.

Clearly, estimating a job correctly requires knowing how fast you work. If you are starting out, you can only guess, but by keeping consistent records, you can quickly begin refining estimates to match the way you really work.

# 5. RECORD-KEEPING

You can track services rendered or pieces delivered, revenues, accounts receivable and overdue payments on one form. It could be a record book divided into columns, an unused checkbook register, or a spreadsheet on a computer. It is important to keep the design simple and easy to use.

Some typical columns for the record or spreadsheet might be:

- Job or Contract Number
- Date delivered
- Rate quoted or billed
- Piece count (words, pages, copies, items, etc.)
- Hours
- Revenue (product of rate times piece count or hours)
- Revenue per hour (Am I above my break-even point?)
- Pieces per hour (How fast am I working?)
- Notes (the type of work, etc.)

You may put a summary row along the bottom that tracks your performance to date. It would contain the sums of the "Piece count," "Revenue" and "Hours" columns. Generate the numbers on the summary line under "$$/hour" and "pieces per hour" from the appropriate items on the summary row, not from the data in the columns above them.

The "Notes" column can help you to refine your piece-rate for different types of work.

A record like this answers questions such as "How many pages do I write per year?" or "How fast do I translate medical journals or lease contracts?" This sheet also contains the gross sales revenue numbers you need for your income tax return or local business taxes.

| job # | date | rate | piece count | revenue | hours | $$/hr | pieces/ hour | notes |
|---|---|---|---|---|---|---|---|---|
| BX0197 | 1/25 | .25 | 200 | $ 50.00 | 1.75 | $ 28.57 | 114.29 | formatting |
| ATD0397 | 1/30 | .25 | 750 | $ 187.50 | 2.5 | $ 75.00 | 300 | boilerplate |
| MCB0197 | 2/1 | .25 | 500 | $ 125.00 | 4.75 | $ 26.32 | 105.26 | lots of lookup |
| MMR1296 | 3/1 | .15 | 25000 | $ 3750.00 | 148 | $ 25.34 | 168.92 | boilerplate |
| | | | | | | | | |
| ~~~ | ~~~ | ~~~ | ~~~ | ~~~ | ~~~ | ~~~ | ~~~ | ~~~ |
| Summary | | .24 | 55253 | $ 13260.72 | 511 | $ 25.95 | 108.13 | |

Table 3 – Excerpt from a sales record.

# 6. DIGITAL HELP

THERE ARE SOFTWARE PROGRAMS to help you track your business. Some are free; many are affordable; all count as a business expense. Be sure to pick one that was designed for your business or that you can customize easily. The steps covered in this book can be done with paper, or a word-processing and spreadsheet package, like Microsoft Office®, Open Office, etc.

Your professional or trade association may have links to tailored products developed by and for your colleagues. The discounts on these programs are among the advantages of belonging to (and networking through) an association.

Personal accounting programs like Quicken® and the packages available from banks and credit unions contain many features to integrate your accounting with your estimates and invoices. Use "personal accounting software" in a search engine (e.g., Google, Yahoo!, Bing) to find free-standing and cloud software products. Many products come with versions for smartphones and other mobile devices.

Remember to build the time to learn new software into its cost when adding it to your budget. Learning curves add to the overhead.

# 7. CONCLUSION

THE COSTING METHOD outlined above should help you determine a break-even point for your work. Many variations are possible, and you should adjust the forms to suit your work style and personal requirements.

The sales record lets you track sales volume and revenue, as well as hourly rates and piece rates coming in from the work. This will support tax reporting and business decision-making.

Many freelancers also work at something else, which is often our main job. We enrich our lives by pursuing multiple activities in parallel. The technical specialization of our other work may be the source of our expertise as a freelancer. Regardless of other sources of income, however, freelancers are in business. To succeed, entrepreneurs must have a passion for their work. Like entrepreneurs, we must pay attention to the bottom line to ensure that we can continue to do the work we love.

Made in the USA
Middletown, DE
05 November 2026

36544976R00023